The Old Cabin in the Forest

Story by Annette Smith

Illustrations by Richard Hoit

Zack and his friend Mitch
were going riding with Zack's parents.

"We have decided to ride
up to the old cabin,
in the forest by the river,"
Zack said to Mitch.
"It's a great place!"

"Does anyone live there?" asked Mitch.

"Not now," laughed Zack.
"But I think wild cats
hide under it sometimes."

Soon they were ready.
They set off along the river path.

"Zack!" shouted Dad.
"Don't ride too fast.
Don't get too far ahead of us."

"Keep on the path
until you get to the forest,"
called Mom. "Wait for us there."

5

At last, Zack and Mitch reached the place
where the river path ended.
Two different paths led into the forest.

Zack's parents caught up with the boys.
"Which way do we go?" asked Zack.

"Follow the path on the left," said Mom.
"Go past the picnic ground."

"Remember to be careful from now on,"
said Dad, "because there are lots
of ferns and branches
hanging over the path.
We don't want either of you
to have an accident."

After a while, they came to the cabin.
"Can you hear that crying sound?"
asked Mitch.

"I can't hear anything," answered Zack.

"Listen," said Mom,
"I think Mitch is right.
I thought I heard something, too.
It's coming from behind the cabin."

"It might be a wild cat!" said Zack.
"I'm not going around there."

"I'll try to find out what it is,"
said Dad. "You wait here."

A moment later, Dad called out,
"There's a little boy
hiding behind the cabin.
He's cold and frightened."

They all ran to help.

The little boy was still crying.
Mom put her jacket around him
and gave him a hug.
"You are safe now," she said gently.

Then Mom gave the little boy
a chocolate bar, and he stopped crying.
He told them that his name was Danny.

"Why are you out here by yourself,
Danny?" asked Mitch.

"Your mom and dad will be wondering
where you are," said Zack.

"They are at the picnic,"
whispered Danny.
"I wanted to find a pet rabbit
in the forest, but I got lost."

"We have to find your parents
as quickly as we can," said Dad.

Mom lifted Danny onto her bike,
and said to him, "You won't fall off.
I'll hold you tightly."

They made their way slowly
back along the path
toward the picnic ground.

Then they heard some people
calling Danny's name.

Zack and Mitch rode ahead
to let them know that he was safe.

Danny's parents were so glad to see him!

After they left, Mom said,
"Who wants to go up
to the wild cat cabin again?"

"We do!" laughed Zack and Mitch.
And off they all went, back up the path.